# My Life with Scoliosis

WRITTEN BY:
ELSIE GUERRERO

ILLUSTRATED BY:
CLARISSA LIBERTELLI

FORMATTED BY:
JEROME VERNELL JR.

978-1-7327573-5-6

PRINTED IN THE UNITED STATES OF AMERICA.

ELSIE PUBLISHING CO.
WWW.ELSIEGUERRERO.COM

THIS BOOK IS
DEDICATED TO

**TIARRA
EARLS**

## ACKNOWLEDGMENT:

I WOULD LIKE TO ACKNOWLEDGE THOSE DIAGNOSED WITH SCOLIOSIS. YOU ARE NOT ALONE. I HOPE THIS STORY WILL BRING JOY.


## DISCLAIMER:

PLEASE BE AWARE THAT THIS STORY IS ONLY INTENDED TO ILLUSTRATE ONE PERSON'S LIFE WITH SCOLIOSIS. OTHERS DIAGNOSED WITH SCOLIOSIS MAY HAVE A DIFFERENT EXPERIENCE.

HELLO! MY NAME IS BEATRIZ AND
I HAVE SCOLIOSIS!

¡HOLA! ¡MI NOMBRE ES BEATRIZ Y
TENGO ESCOLIOSIS!

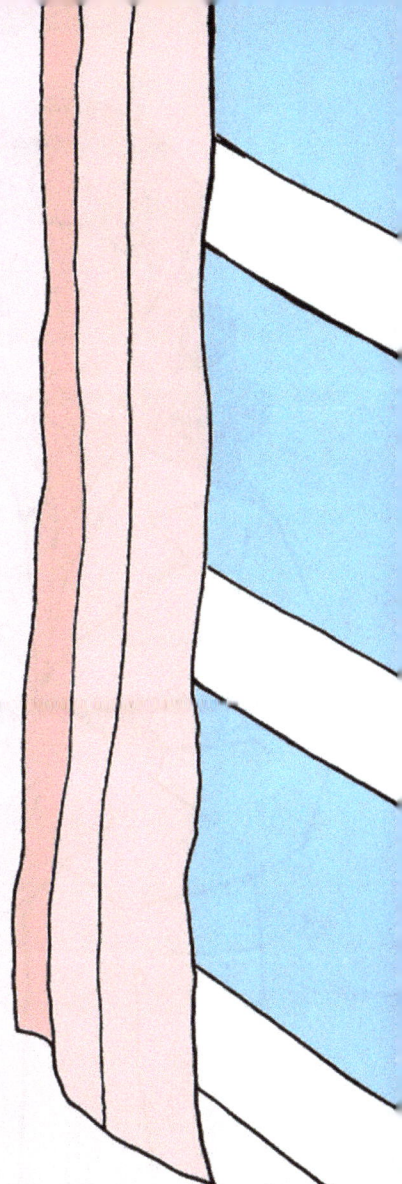

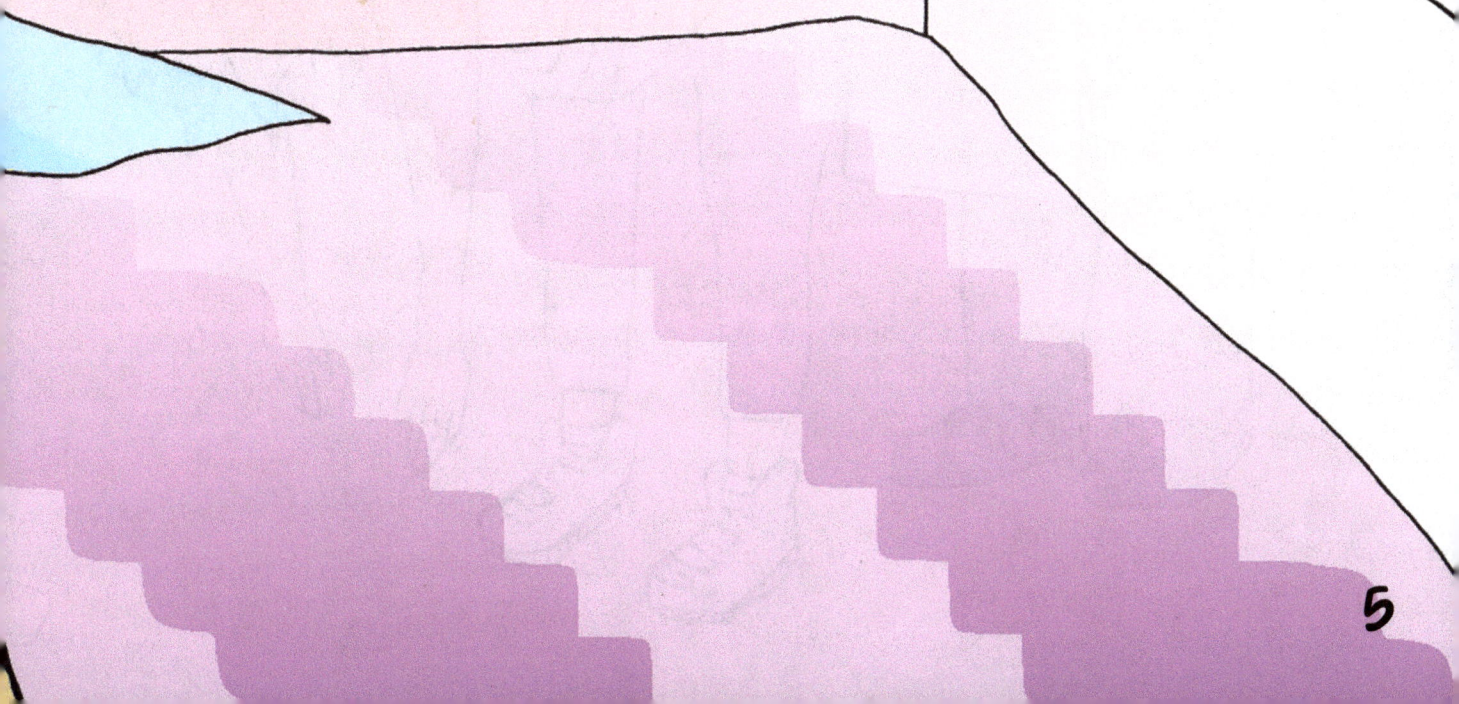

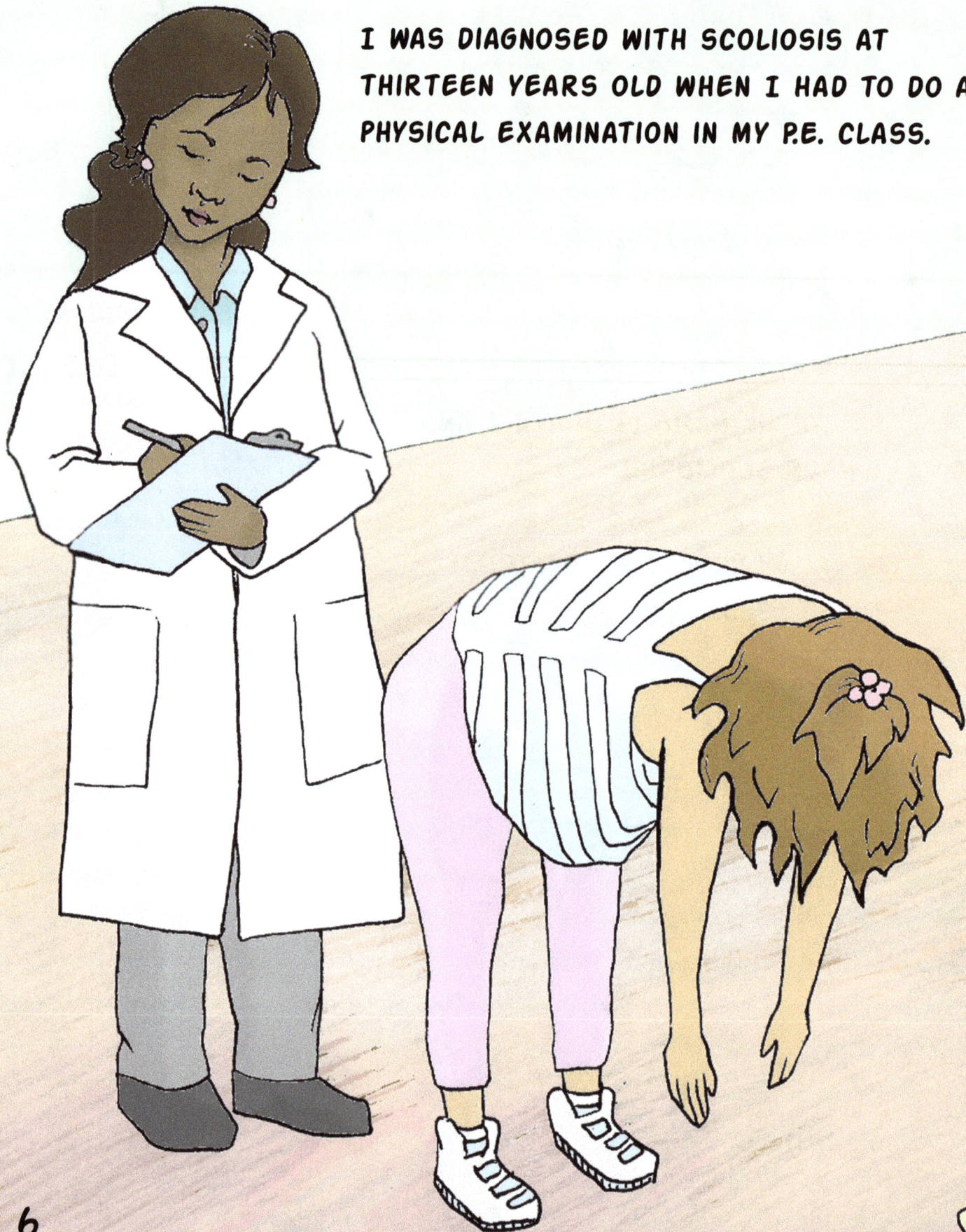

I WAS DIAGNOSED WITH SCOLIOSIS AT THIRTEEN YEARS OLD WHEN I HAD TO DO A PHYSICAL EXAMINATION IN MY P.E. CLASS.

ME DIAGNOSTICARON ESCOLIOSIS A LOS TRECE AÑOS DE EDAD CUANDO TUVE QUE HACER UN EXAMEN FÍSICO EN MI EDUCACIÓN FÍSICA CLASE.

SCOLIOSIS IS A CONDITION
INVOLVING AN ABNORMAL
SIDEWAYS CURVATURE
OF THE SPINE. STUDIES
HAVE BEEN DONE, BUT NO
CAUSE HAS BEEN FOUND.

LA ESCOLIOSIS ES UNA
CONDICIÓN QUE IMPLICA
UNA CURVATURA
LATERAL ANORMAL
DE LA COLUMNA
VERTEBRAL. SE HAN
REALIZADO ESTUDIOS,
PERO NO SE HAN
ENCONTRADO CAUSAS.

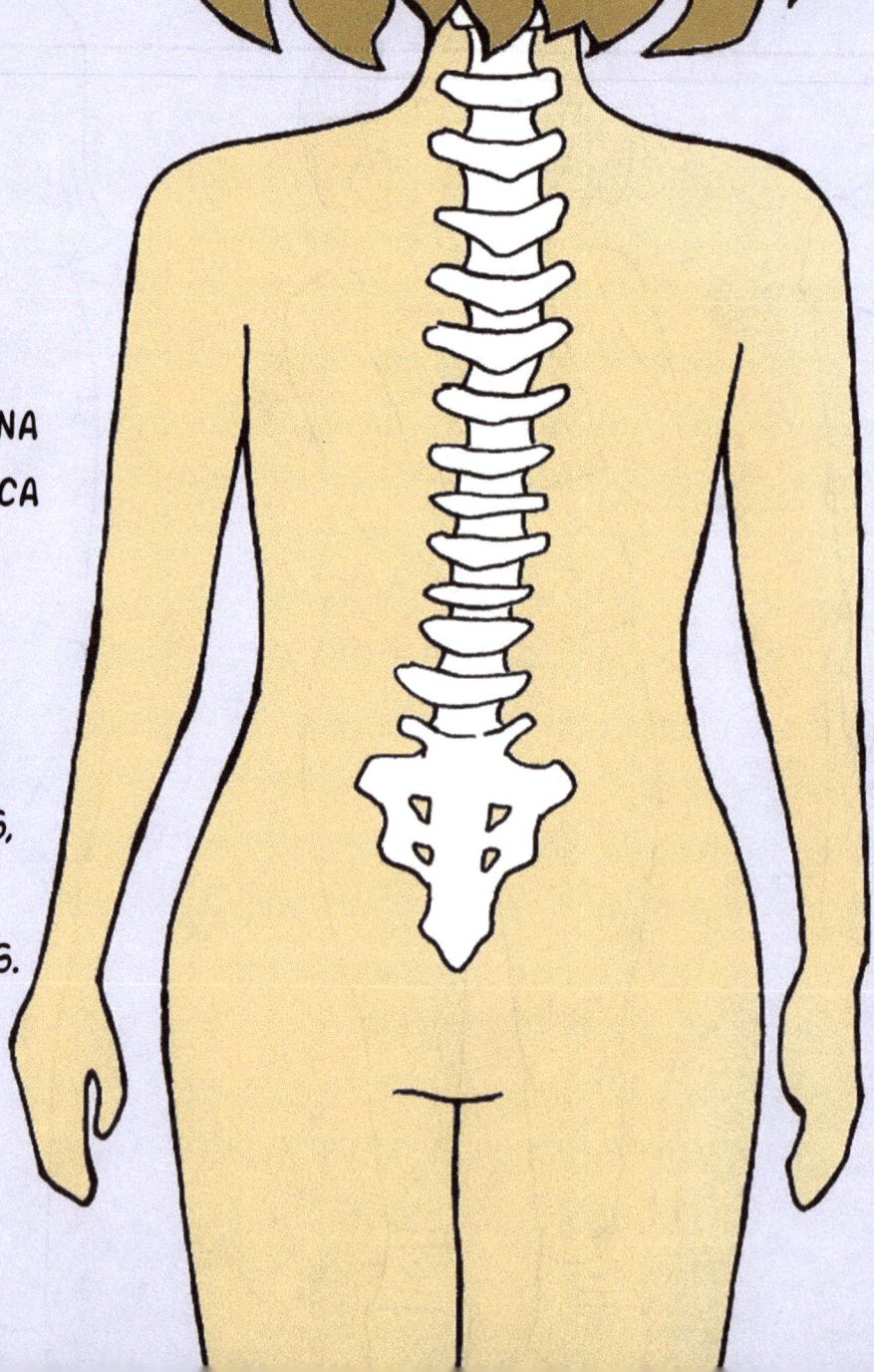

8

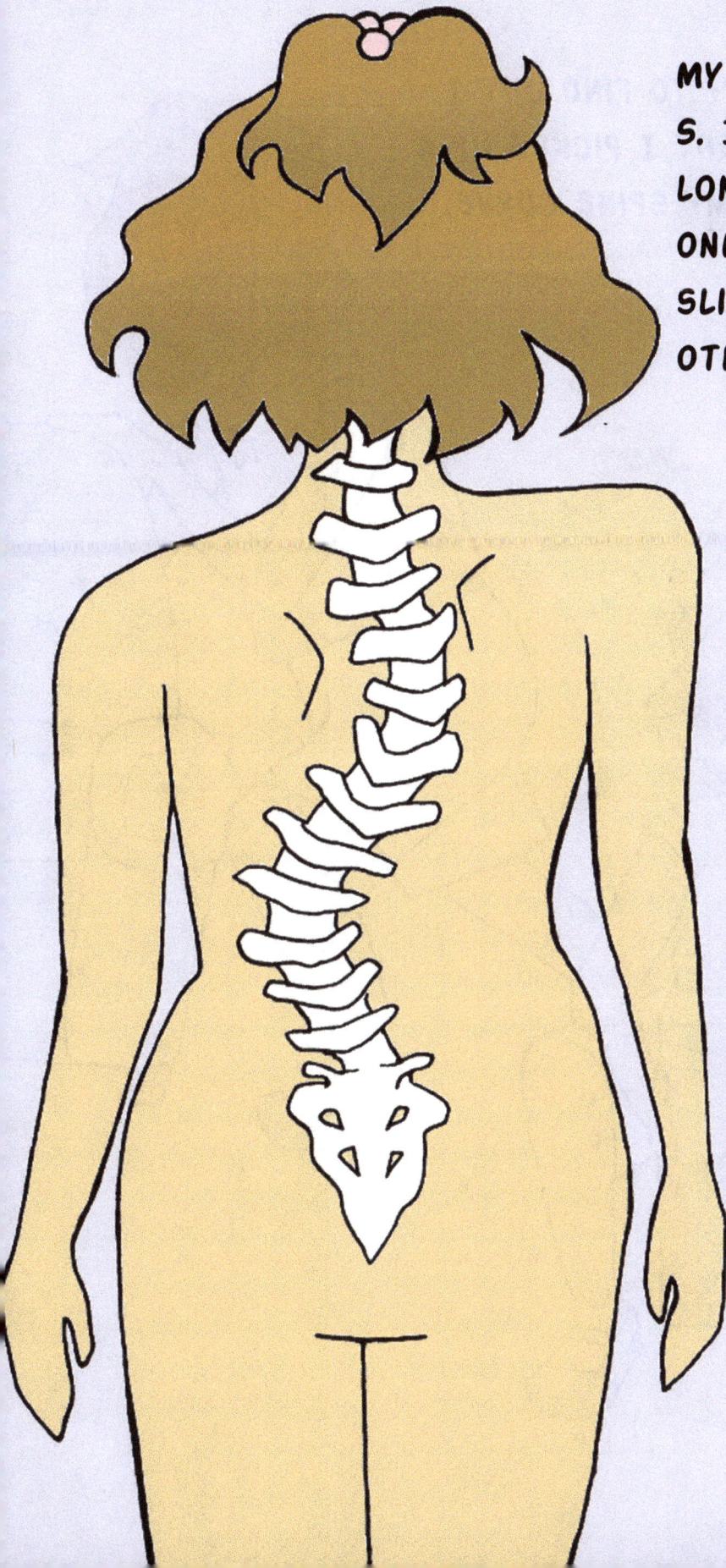

MY SPINE IS SHAPE LIKE AN S. I HAVE ONE LEG SLIGHTLY LONGER THAN THE OTHER ONE AND ONE SHOULDER IS SLIGHTLY HIGHER THAN THE OTHER ONE.

MI COLUMNA VERTEBRAL TIENE FORMA DE S. TENGO UNA PIERNA UN POCO MÁS LARGA QUE LA OTRA Y UN HOMBRO ES LIGERAMENTE MÁS ALTO QUE LA OTRA.

9

MY MOTHER WAS NOT HAPPY TO FIND OUT I HAD SCOLIOSIS. SHE THOUGHT I PICKED UP A HEAVY OBJECT AND MADE MY SPINE CURVE.

MI MADRE NO ESTABA FELIZ DE SABER QUE TENÍA
ESCOLIOSIS. ELLA PENSÓ QUE RECOGÍ UN OBJETO
PESADO E HICE MI CURVA DE COLUMNA VERTEBRAL.

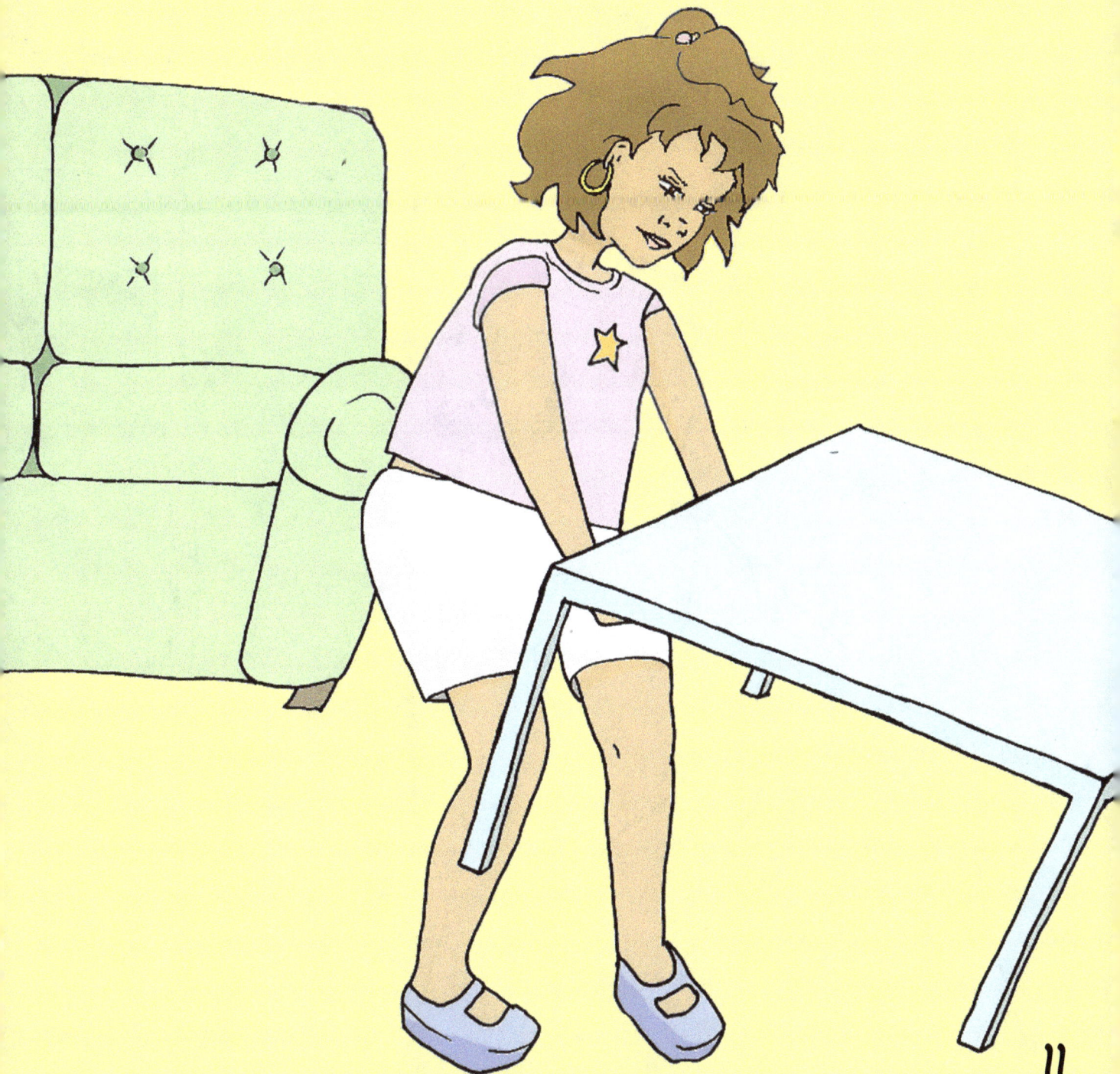

SINCE MY MOTHER THOUGHT I PURPOSELY MADE MY SPINE CURVE, SHE MADE ME DO MANY THINGS TO FIX MY BACK.

DESDE QUE MI MADRE PENSÓ QUE HICE MI CURVA DE COLUMNA A PROPÓSITO, ME OBLIGÓ A HACER MUCHAS COSAS PARA ARREGLAR MI ESPALDA.

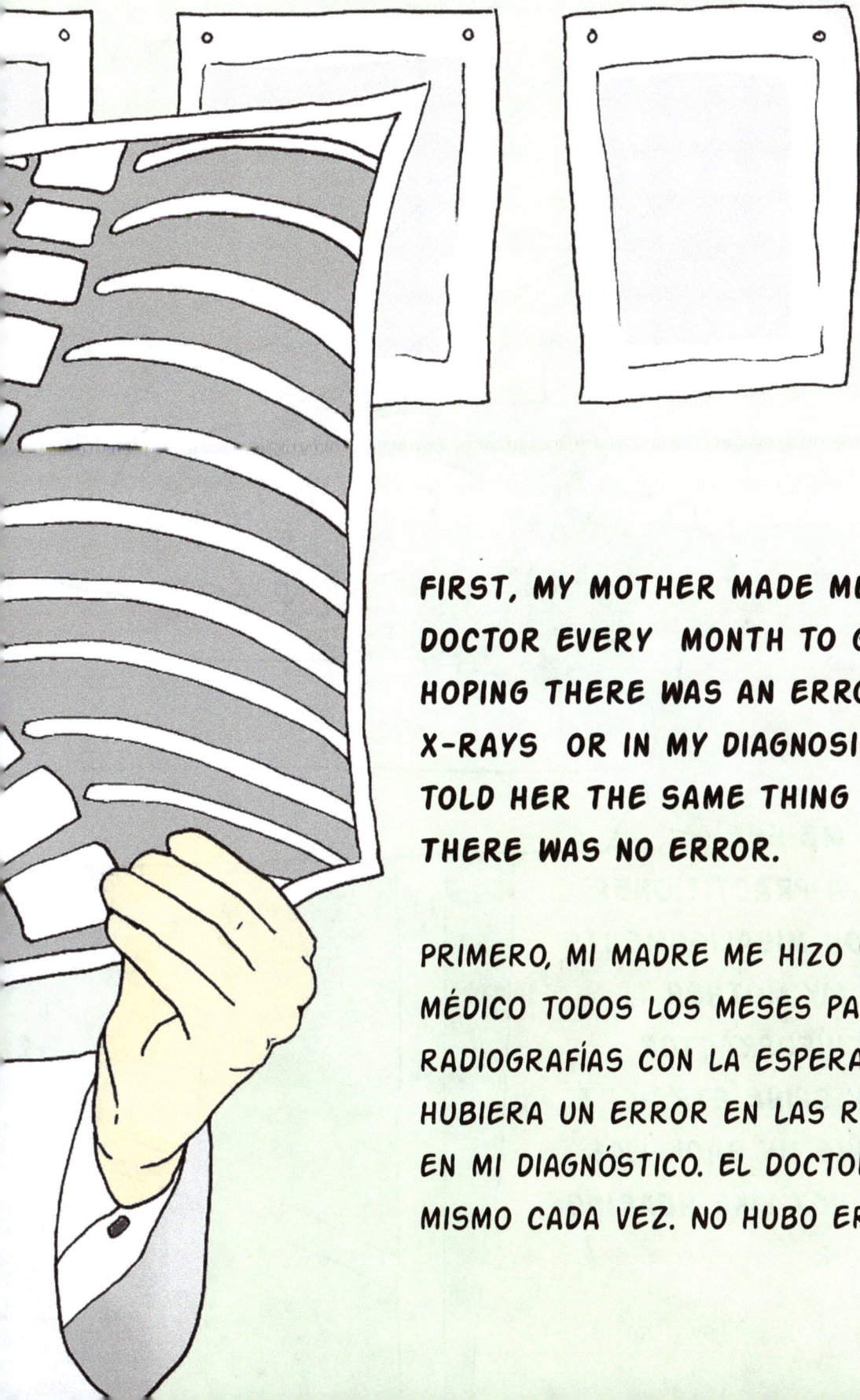

FIRST, MY MOTHER MADE ME SEE THE
DOCTOR EVERY MONTH TO GET X-RAYS
HOPING THERE WAS AN ERROR IN THE
X-RAYS OR IN MY DIAGNOSIS. THE DOCTOR
TOLD HER THE SAME THING EVERY TIME.
THERE WAS NO ERROR.

PRIMERO, MI MADRE ME HIZO VER AL
MÉDICO TODOS LOS MESES PARA OBTENER
RADIOGRAFÍAS CON LA ESPERANZA DE QUE
HUBIERA UN ERROR EN LAS RADIOGRAFÍAS O
EN MI DIAGNÓSTICO. EL DOCTOR LE DECÍA LO
MISMO CADA VEZ. NO HUBO ERROR.

13

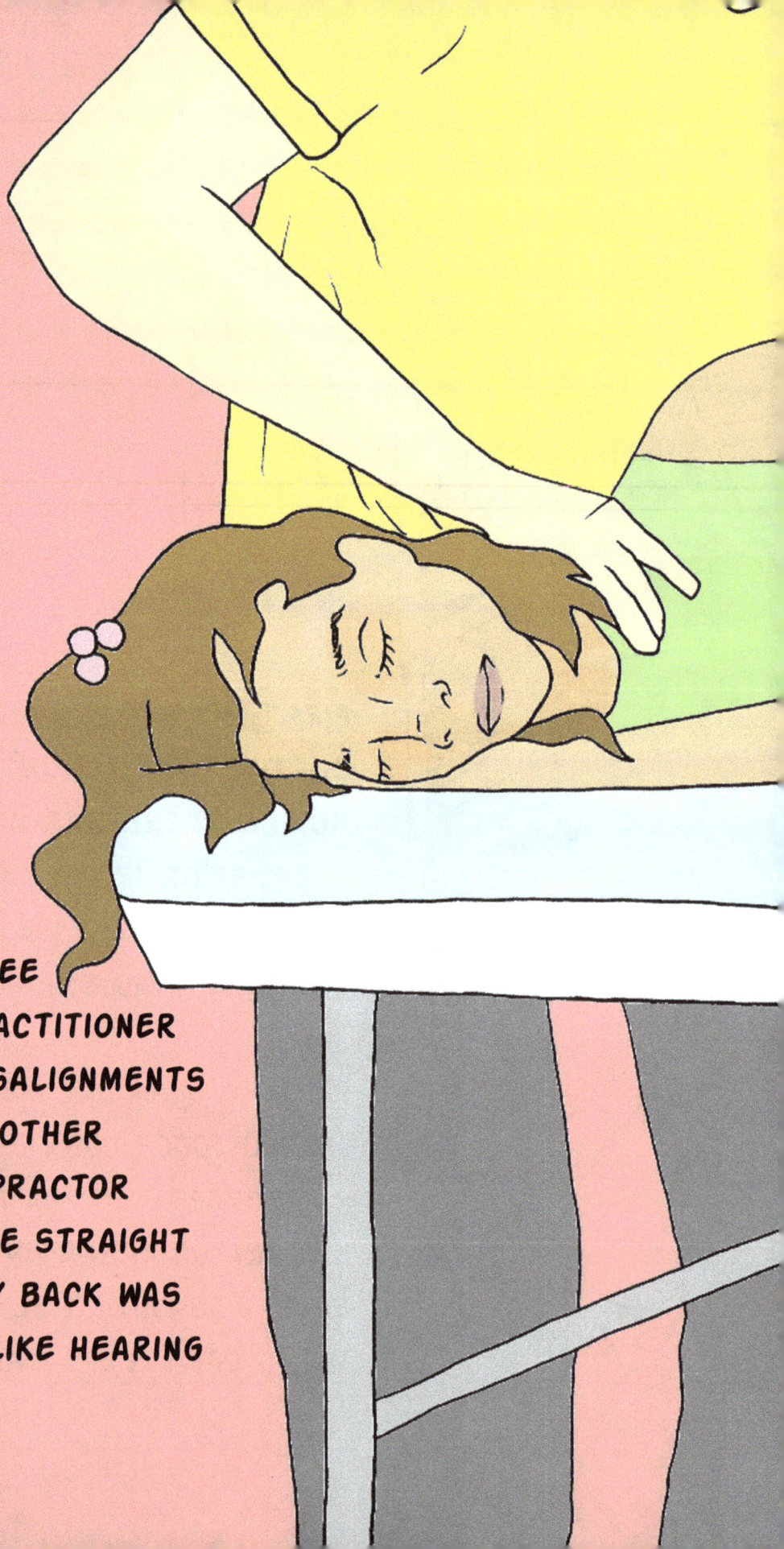

THEN, SHE HAD ME SEE
CHIROPRACTOR, A PRACTITIONER
WHO FOCUSES ON MISALIGNMENTS
OF THE BONES. MY MOTHER
THOUGHT THE CHIROPRACTOR
COULD MAKE MY SPINE STRAIGHT
AGAIN. ADJUSTING MY BACK WAS
NOT FUN. I DID NOT LIKE HEARING
MY BONES CRACK.

14

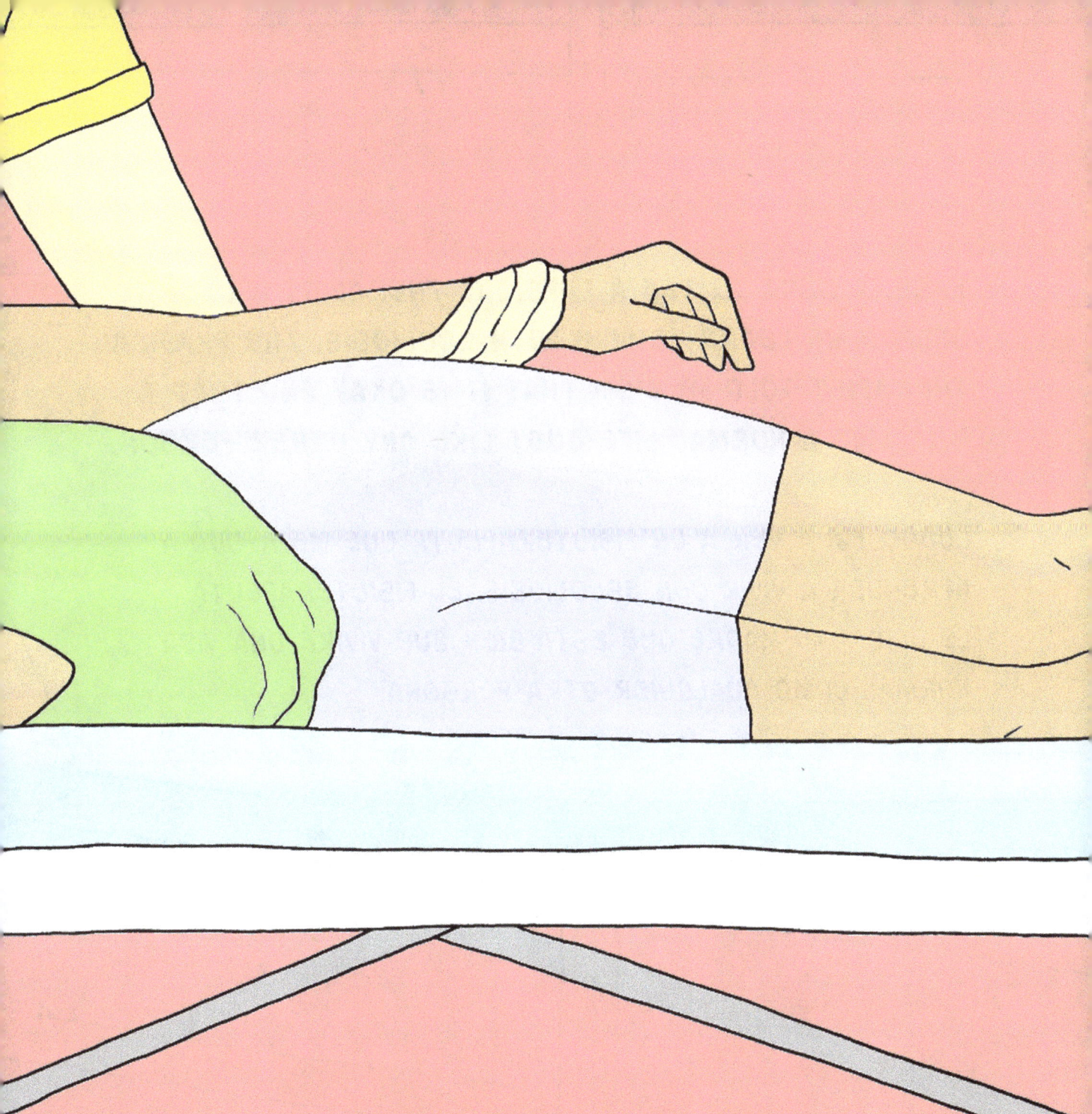

ENTONCES, ELLA ME HIZO VER A UN QUIROPRÁCTICO, UN PRACTICANTE
QUE SE ENFOCA EN LOS DESAJUSTES DE LOS HUESOS. MI MADRE
PENSÓ QUE EL QUIROPRÁCTICO PODRÍA ENDEREZAR MI COLUMNA
VERTEBRAL DE NUEVO. AJUSTAR MI ESPALDA NO FUE DIVERTIDO. NO
ME GUSTABA ESCUCHAR MIS HUESOS CRUJIR.

THEN, I WENT TO SEE A PHYSICAL THERAPIST WHO HELPED ME LEARN TO LIVE WITH SCOLIOSIS. THE PHYSICAL THERAPIST TOLD MY MOM THAT IT IS OKAY AND THAT I WILL LIVE A NORMAL LIFE JUST LIKE ANY OTHER PERSON.

LUEGO, FUI A VER A UN FISIOTERAPEUTA QUE ME AYUDÓ A APRENDER A VIVIR CON ESCOLIOSIS. EL FISIOTERAPEUTA LE DIJO A MI MADRE QUE ESTÁ BIEN QUE VIVIRÉ UNA VIDA NORMAL COMO CUALQUIER OTRA PERSONA.

ALTHOUGH I DID PHYSICAL THERAPY, SOMETIMES I GET STRONG BACK PAIN THAT ONLY GETS BETTER WHEN I LAY ON THE FLOOR.

AUNQUE HICE TERAPIA FÍSICA, A VECES ME DOLÍA MUCHO
LA ESPALDA Y TENÍA QUE TUMBARME EN EL SUELO PARA
QUE ME SINTIERA MEJOR.

19

I EVEN HAD TO WEAR A BACK BRACE FOR A FEW MONTHS AT NIGHT WHEN I WAS FIRST DIAGNOSED WITH SCOLIOSIS TO TREAT THE CURVATURE OF THE SPINE.

INCLUSO TUVE QUE USAR UN REFUERZO EN LA ESPALDA DURANTE ALGUNOS MESES EN LA NOCHE CUANDO ME DIAGNOSTICARON ESCOLIOSIS PARA TRATAR LA CURVATURA DE LA COLUMNA VERTEBRAL.

HOWEVER, MY SCOLIOSIS HAS NEVER PREVENTED ME FROM DANCING, PLAYING SPORTS OR LIVING A LIFE LIKE ANY OTHER KID MY AGE.

SIN EMBARGO, MI ESCOLIOSIS NUNCA ME HA
IMPEDIDO BAILAR, PRACTICAR DEPORTES O
VIVIR UNA VIDA COMO LA DE CUALQUIER OTRO
NIÑO DE MI EDAD.

23

MY MOTHER EVENTUALLY ACCEPTED ME FOR WHO I AM AND LEARNED THAT I AM NOT DIFFERENT, BUT UNIQUE IN MY OWN WAY. I LOVE WHO I AM. HAVING SCOLIOSIS MAKES ME UNIQUE AND I LOVE IT!

MI MADRE FINALMENTE ME ACEPTÓ POR LO QUE SOY Y APRENDÍ QUE NO SOY DIFERENTE, SINO ÚNICA A MI MANERA. ME ENCANTA QUIEN SOY. TENER ESCOLIOSIS ME HACE ÚNICO Y ME ENCANTA!

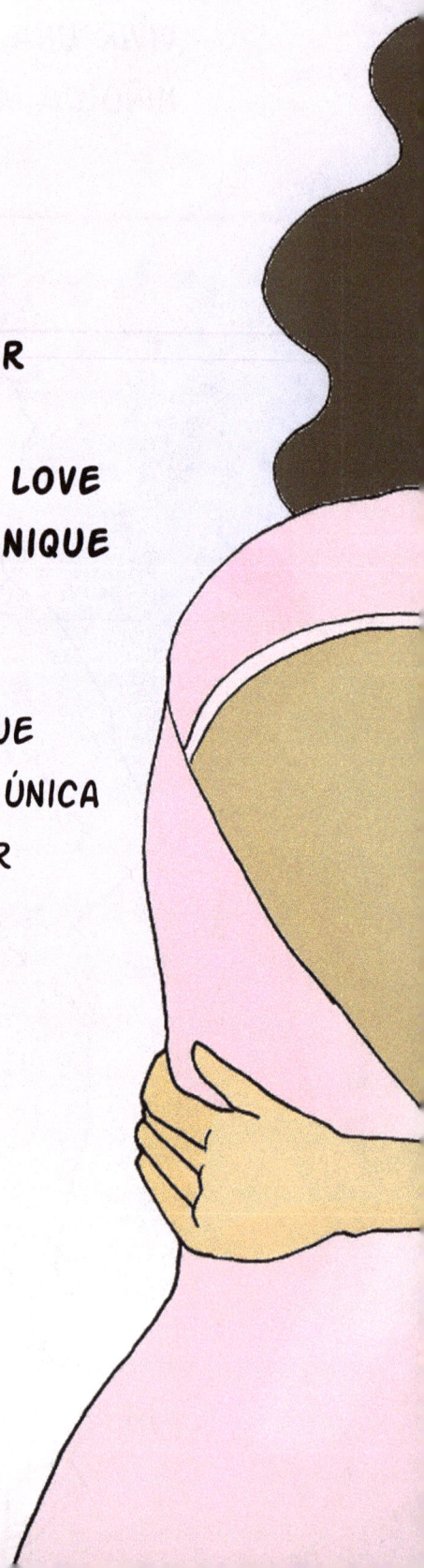

ELSIE GUERRERO IS THE AUTHOR OF HOW EMILY AND ELI BECAME FRIENDS, THE BEAUTY IN ME AND I AM UNIQUE. ELSIE HAS BEEN WORKING WITH CHILDREN WITH SPECIAL NEEDS SINCE 2011. HER EXPOSURE AND EXPERIENCE WORKING WITH CHILDREN WITH SPECIAL NEEDS INSPIRED HER TO WRITE ABOUT THEIR LIVES TO SPREAD AWARENESS AND PROMOTE INCLUSION.

# LIKE MY LIFE WITH SCOLIOSIS? CHECK OUT OTHER BOOKS WRITTEN BY ELSIE GUERRERO.

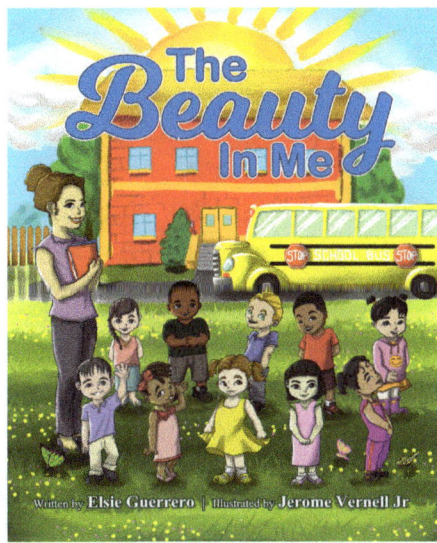

The Beauty In Me — Written by Elsie Guerrero | Illustrated by Jerome Vernell Jr.

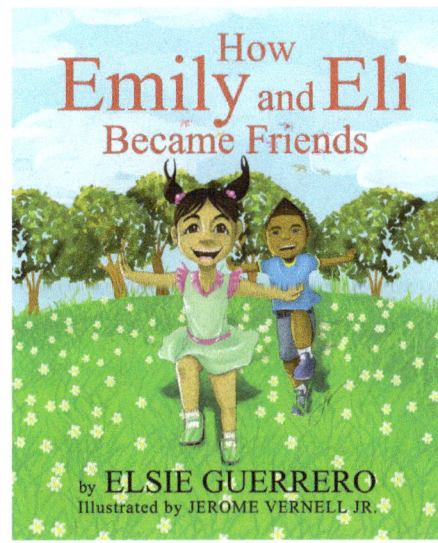

How Emily and Eli Became Friends — by ELSIE GUERRERO, Illustrated by JEROME VERNELL JR.

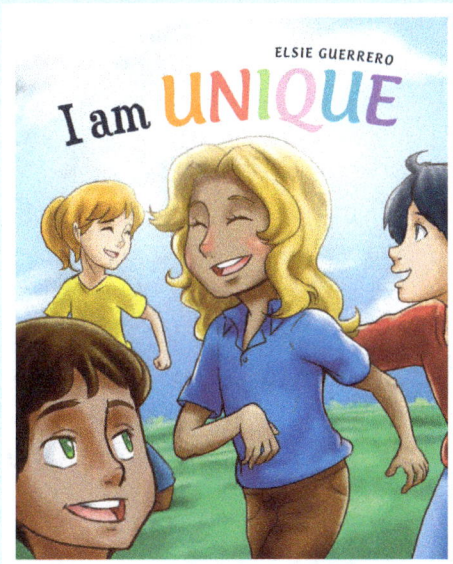

I am UNIQUE — ELSIE GUERRERO

Dancing Luna — ELSIE GUERRERO, Illustrated by Harriet Kim and Rodis

# SPREAD AWARENESS. PROMOTE INCLUSION.

www.ingramcontent.com/pod-product-compliance
Lightning Source LLC
Chambersburg PA
CBHW062013090426
42811CB00005B/835